Easy Piano

CD Included

GRAND Staff-Capers

A MUSICAL VOYAGE THROUGH THE LINES AND SPACES

By Cynthia Pace

CONTENTS

© Copyright 2008 by Cynthia Pace
Music, words, arrangements by Cynthia Pace. International copyright secured.
ALL RIGHTS RESERVED. Unauthorized copying, arranging, adapting, or
recording is an infringement of copyright. Infringers are liable under the law.

Lee Roberts Music Publications Inc.
Chatham, New York

DISTRIBUTED BY

HAL•LEONARD CORPORATION
7777 W. BLUEMOUND RD. P.O. BOX 13819 MILWAUKEE, WI 53212

About
GRAND STAFF-CAPERS
- A Musical Voyage through the Lines and Spaces -

The short, lively, and easy-to-master selections in this book offer beginning piano students musical experience that is entertaining as well as rewarding. Each selection in this companion book to the Robert Pace Keyboard Series reinforces concepts of the core books, providing:

- PRACTICE in line, space, and pattern recognition; in performance of basic rhythms; and in identification of these rhythms both by sight and by sound;
- A sparking of the student's IMAGINATION, as the student is guided to expand upon each piece in this collection, and create his or her own IMPROVISATIONS and COMPOSITIONS;
- LASTING FUN, because the reinforcement of READING, WRITING, and LISTENING SKILLS supports ongoing musical learning and enjoyment.

The selections in this book also remind students that the treble and bass clefs "belong" to both hands -- each hand may play in either clef, according to the music. ALL of the LINES and SPACES of the grand staff, from "E" below the bass clef, to "A" above the treble, plus a variety of tonalities, are sampled in this whimsical musical voyage.

The CD contained in this book serves many helpful functions such as:

- MODELING the music;
- Offering students "ENSEMBLE" playing experience;
- Providing a BACKDROP for creative IMPROVISATIONS.

The CD furnishes three or more tracks for each *Staff-Capers* composition, in this order:

1. Composition played at very slow, PRACTICE TEMPO;
2. Composition played up to tempo with INSTRUMENTAL ACCOMPANIMENT;
3. Accompaniment track for IMPROVISATION, repeated 3 times. Claves/wood blocks play rhythm of the related composition the first two times through.

An index of CD Tracks appears on page 18.

Rhythm Pattern Cards are included on Pages 19-24 of this book.

Since rhythm is the "backbone" of music, reinforcing skill in reading, writing, hearing, and performing rhythmic patterns enhances students' all-around musical experience and facility. Toward this end, key rhythmic patterns from each piece in this book are printed in the back of the book. Students may cut these out as flashcards to practice as each new piece is begun. Basic flashcard activities might include:

- CLAPPING the RHYTHMIC PATTERN while saying the notes' rhythmics names ("H-a-l-f --N-o-t-e, quar-ter," etc.);
- Clapping along with the corresponding CD track to check for accuracy (see CD tracks/rhythms list, page 18);
- Arranging cards (from both current and preceding selections in the book) in different orders across a music stand, and CLAPPING this "COMPOSITION;"
- PLAYING the "COMPOSITION" on any notes of the keyboard;
- Playing the "composition" with other RHYTHM INSTRUMENTS.

These activities can be especially enjoyable when several students work together.

"At-Home" Rhythmic Dictation using CD: Because each rhythm card has a corresponding CD track (see page 18), students can practice rhythmic "dictation" at home. For instance, the student, or a helper, might play a track so that the student can listen and try to correctly write the rhythm that is heard. Answers may then be checked with the CD track index.

LEARNING SUGGESTIONS: *Staff-Capers* first presents a musical selection, follows with improvisation instructions, and, after that, with composition instructions. Strict adherence to this sequence is not necessary, however. Rather, the material in this book may be adapted for many different situations and needs. (It should be noted that these selections are ordered by level of difficulty.) Following are some suggestions, for use as needed:

Beginning New Music:

In addition to practicing rhythms with cards and CD tracks, students may also:

1. LISTEN to the CD slow-tempo performance of a new composition while FOLLOWING the NOTES in the music;
2. Say the WORDS to the music, or chant the notes' RHYTHMIC NAMES, while CLAPPING the rhythm;
3. Listen to and "SHAPE" the melody. Move horizontally held hand up or down "in the air," in relation to how the melody moves. Say "step," "skip," or "same" to indicate the direction the melody moves;
4. Say/sing the LETTER-NAMES of the notes while watching the music;
5. POSITION hands on keys indicated by hand-position diagram, and play new piece slowly. Keep eyes on the page, not on the keyboard, when first learning a composition;
6. PRACTICE the piece several times. Then, play along with the slow practice CD track;
7. Repeat this a few times. Following this, work without the CD, and gradually increase the tempo of the piece;
8. After becoming comfortable playing the piece at a moderate speed, begin trying to play along with the faster CD track. Try to keep going despite any "missed" notes. Go back to a slower tempo without CD, periodically. (Practicing with a friend is helpful. For instance, one person can play the part for one hand, while the other plays the other part. Or, both people can play the same part together, one person playing at a higher or lower register than written.)

HINTS FOR "CREATIVE SUCCESS:"

Improvisation "versus" Composition: Improvising and composing are, of course, intertwined. At the same time, their differences influence how each art is learned. Improvisation involves the skill of "making it up on the fly." Maintaining forward momentum in real time is key. Composing, on the other hand, tends to involve a lot of starting and stopping, consideration and reconsideration, tweaking and changing a little bit at a time.

Improvising -- To learn the central skill of "thinking in musical motion," students should:

- PLAY STRAIGHT THROUGH their improvisations and avoid stopping in the middle to correct "mistakes." Maintaining the rhythm, even if the notes are not perfect, is important in starting out.
- Practice improvising frequently. Sometimes, improvise at a slower tempo, to get time to think and "clean up" an improvisation.
- Be patient -- Trial-and-error is part of the creative process!

Composing -- Students will find it helpful to:

- Play and listen frequently to the music they write down, as they are working on it.
- Try changing some notes to other notes. If these sound "better," write them in place of the original notes. Use a pencil so changes may be made easily.

And now, on to some Grand-Staff Capers.....

4

Rhythm Pattern Cut-Outs 1-6 (pg 19)
CD Tracks 1-7 : No. 1--slow practice,
2--regular tempo with accompaniment,
3-7--see directions for improvisation, pg 5.

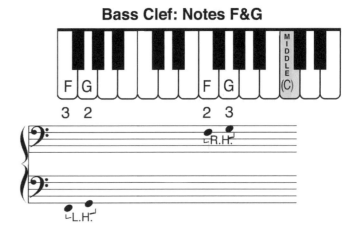

Cut out and practice
Rhythm Pattern Cards 1-6
(pg 19), then practice *Chris*
(see suggestions, pgs 2-3).

Chris the Rhinoceros

Hey there, my | name is "Chris," I'm | known for two horns on my | pro - bos - cis. In

Chris ends on its keynote, "G." Ending on the keynote makes a song sound "complete."

mud I splash, I'm | fast when I dash, and | when I'm with my friends, our | group is called a "crash!"

"Proboscis" means nose.

Additional Options: Practice identifying and playing "F" and "G," along with other notes, using *Robert Pace Lines and Spaces Flashcards* (available through your music dealer, or at: leerobertsmusic.com).

Improvise. PRIOR TO USING THE CD: 1. Clap the rhythm of *Chris*, as you say the words to the song. 2. Play the song's rhythm on the piano a few times, using keynote "G." 3. Position your hands on the keys used for playing "Chis," and play tones "F" and "G" in any order, to the rhythm of *Chris*. "Complete" each new melody by ending on the keynote "G." Make up several new melodies. **PLAYING ALONG WITH CD: Trk 3:** The claves repeat only the phrase "Hey there, my name is "Chris," over and over, four times. Along with this track, play "F" and "G" in any new order, in time to the claves' rhythm. Avoid stopping in the middle to correct "mistakes." **Trk 4:** The claves repeat only the phrase "I'm known for two horns on my proboscis." Play "F" and "G" in any new order, in time to this rhythm. **Trk 5:** Do as before, this time with the phrase "In mud I splash, I'm fast when I dash." **Trk 6:** Do as before, now with the phrase "and when I'm with my friends, our group is called a 'crash!'" **Trk 7:** Play "F" and "G" in any order, along with the rhythm to the entire song. When this becomes easy, play "F" and "G" in your own, new rhythms. Finally, you may wish to expand to using any notes from the full mixolydian mode of "G," "A," "B," "C," "D," "E," and "F."

Write a new song: Choose from the SAME SET of TONES, "F" and "G," that are used in *Chris*. Write these tones below, in any NEW order you wish. Use the SAME RHYTHM that *Chris* uses. This rhythm appears in light print.

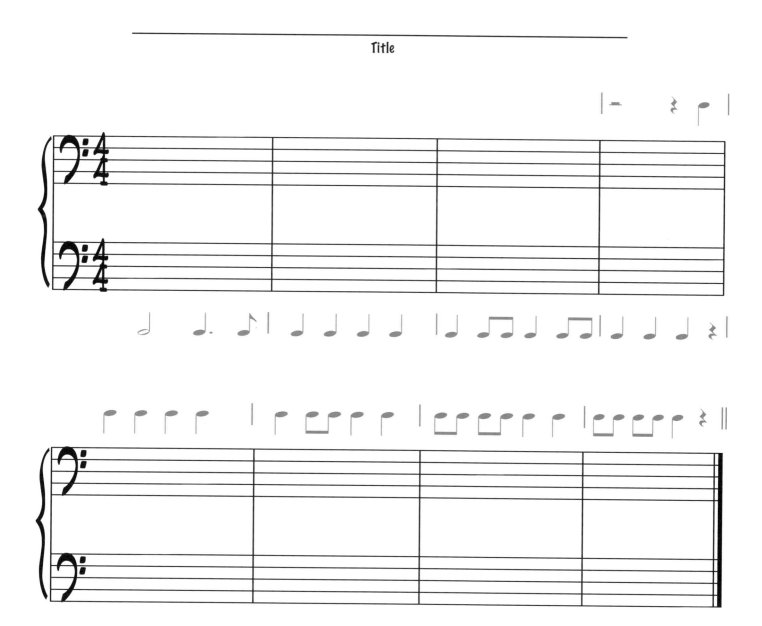

Title

End on the note "G" to make your new song sound "complete."

6

Treble Clef: D Dorian Tones

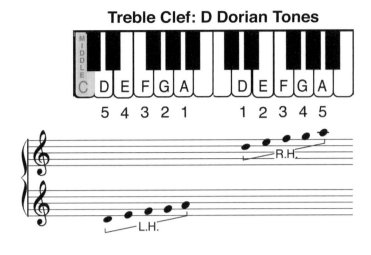

Unicorn

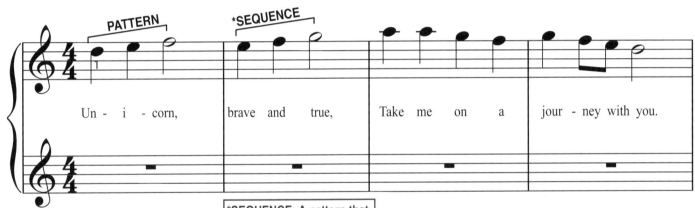

PATTERN   *SEQUENCE

Un - i - corn, | brave and true, | Take me on a | jour - ney with you.

*SEQUENCE: A pattern that repeats on different keys.

Show me pla - ces | you like to roam, | Show me where you | make your __ home.

5

Unicorn ends on its keynote, "D."

Good Gizzards! Measures 5-8 REPEAT measures 1-4 almost exactly!

Improvise New Melodies: 1. Clap the rhythm of *Unicorn*, as you say the words to the song. 2. Play the song's rhythm on the piano a few times, using keynote "D." 3. Position your hands on the keys used for playing *Unicorn*, and play tones "D," "E," "F," "G," and "A" in any new order. Use the rhythm of *Unicorn*. "Complete" each new melody by ending on the keynote "D." Make up several new melodies. 4. Play **CD Track 10,** and repeat steps 1, 2 and 3, as the accompaniment plays.

Write a New Song: Choose from tones "D," "E," "F," "G," and "A" that are used in *Unicorn.* Write these tones below, in a new order. Use the same rhythm that *Unicorn* uses. You may wish to try RE-PEATING measures 1-4 of your composition in measures 5-8.

Rhythm Pattern Cut-Outs 9-11 (pg 21)
CD Tracks 11-13

Pentatonic Scale Tones

Musical Question and Answers: Measures 1-4 of *Kiai!* form a musical "question." Measures 5-8 form an "answer." Listen to this "question and answer," as you play *Kiai!*

Parallel and Contrasting Question and Answers: Musical answers that begin like the question, are "PARALLEL ANSWERS." Answers that begin differently than the question, are "CONTRASTING ANSWERS." Which kind of answer does *Kiai!* use?

Kiai!

Additional Options: Practice identifying and playing flatted and sharped notes, using *Robert Pace Chromatic Lines and Spaces Flashcards* (available through your music dealer, or at: leerobertsmusic.com).

Improvise New Melodies: 1. Clap in time to the notes of *Kiai!*, as you say the notes' rhythmic names ("two-eighths, eighth, eighth, h-a-l-f--n-o-t-e," etc. 2. Play the song's rhythm on the piano a few times, using keynote "E♭." 3. Position your hands on the keys used for playing *Kiai!* Choose from tones "G♭," "A♭," "B♭," "D♭," and "E♭," and play any of these you like, as you follow the rhythm for *Kiai!* Complete each new melody by ending on the keynote "E♭." Make up several new melodies. 4. Play **CD Track 13,** and repeat steps 1, 2 and 3, as the accompaniment plays.

COMPOSING A QUESTION AND ANSWER.

Create Your Own Question: Choose from tones "G♭," "A♭" "B♭," "D♭," and "E♭" that are used in *Kiai!* Write these tones in a new order, below, in MEASURES 1-4. Use the same rhythm that *Kiai!* uses.

Create Your Own Answer: Now, play some answers that begin just like your question, that is, PARALLEL answers. Then, play some other CONTRASTING answers that begin differently, choosing from tones "G♭," "A♭" "B♭," "D♭," and "E♭." Decide which kind of answer you prefer for your question. Write your musical "answer" in measures 5-8. Use the same rhythm that *Kiai* uses for your answer, then, later, try using new rhythms for other answers, if you wish.

Title

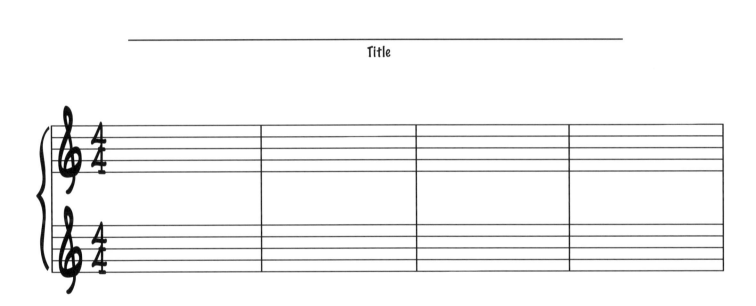

End on "E♭."

Rhythm Pattern Cut-Outs 10 (pg 21)
CD Tracks 14-17

My Dog

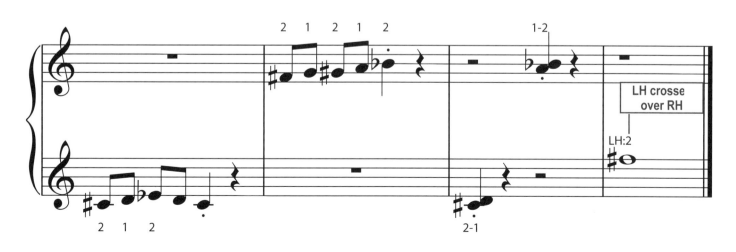

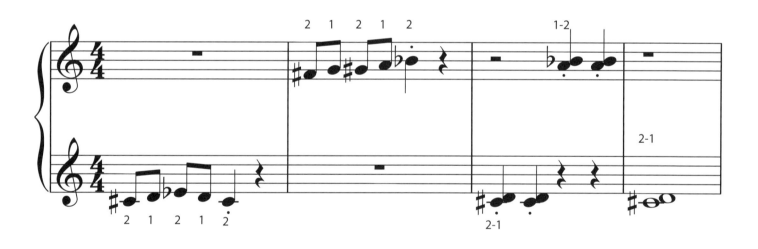

Improvise New Melodies based on the song, *My Dog:* Follow the same procedures you used for improvising on the preceding pages. "Complete" each new melody by ending on the keynote "F#."

Write a New Song: Use the SAME SET of TONES that are used in *My Dog.* Use the SAME RHYTHM as in *My Dog*, or, instead, create your own new 4/4 rhythms.

Title

> Draw your own TREBLE clefs on the staff below.

Rhythm Pattern Cut-Outs 13-15 (pg 21)
CD Tracks 18-20

Sleuth Mouse Detective

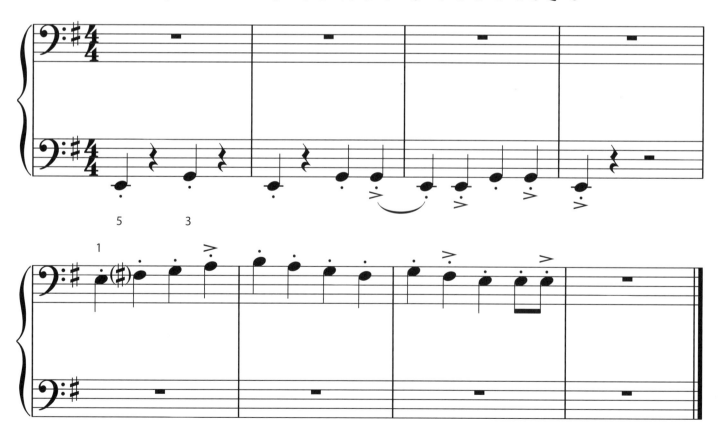

Additional Options: Practice identifying key signatures, using *Robert Pace Key Signature Flashcards* (available through your music dealer, or at: leerobertsmusic.com).

Improvise New Melodies based on *Sleuth Mouse Detective:* Follow the same procedures you used for improvising, on the preceding pages. "Complete" each new melody by ending on the keynote "E." When playing your left hand, you may wish to use notes from the full e-minor Tune-up "E," "F#," "G," "A," and "B" instead of only "E" and "G."

Write a new song: Use the SAME SET of TONES that are used in *Sleuth Mouse Detective*. Also, use the SAME RHYTHM as in *Sleuth Mouse Detective*, or create your own new rhythms.

_____

Title

> **Draw your own BASS clef and sharp on the staff below.**

14

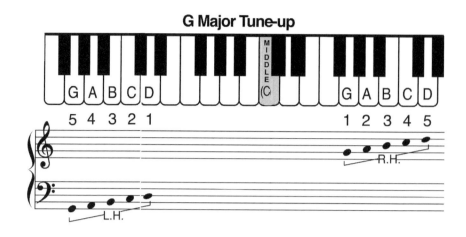

In addition to playing this song on the piano, try singing it as a round with some friends. After the first singer (or group) finishes the first measure, the second singer or group begins their part. All may wish to sing their parts in the same register, each starting from the same "G" (treble clef, line 2).

Song of the Frogs

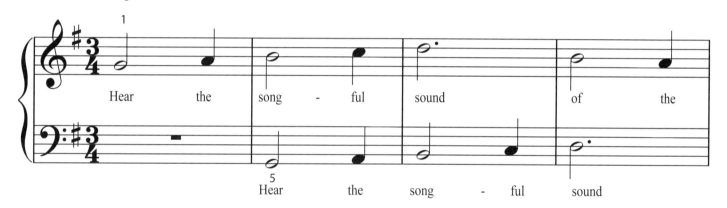

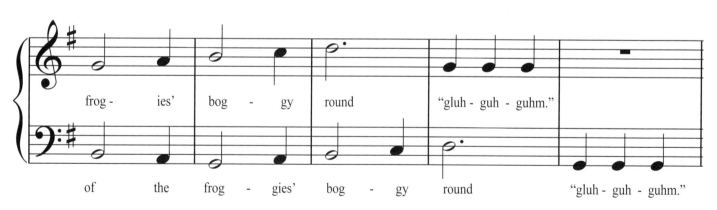

Now, "sing" your own frog sounds and "songs" for four measures' time:

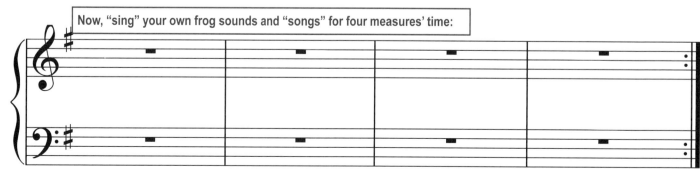

Improvise New Melodies based on Song of the Frogs, in one hand and then the other.

Write a melody in the treble clef for your right hand in measures 1-8. Add words, if you like. Write the same melody in the bass clef for your left hand in measures 9-16 (Repeat the same words, or add new ones). Choose from tones "G," "A," "B," "C," and "D."

Title

Draw the clefs, key signature, and time signature that appear in *Song of the Frogs.*

Optional: Compose a melody that can be played as a round. One hand begins playing the melody, and continues on. The other hand then starts one measure after the first hand begins, playing the same melody, but in a different octave. It takes some experimentation to get a melody that will work well as a round. It is easier to use only notes "G," "B," and "D" (chord tones), to start with. Have a friend help out, playing one part while you play the other.

Creating Your Own Music From "Scratch:"

Now it's time to create some music, using any notes and rhythms in any arrangement you wish. Perhaps you have done this before. One way to get started is to imagine telling a "musical story," or to think of creating a sound track for a movie.

An Example of a Musical Story:

You can hear an example of a musical story, called *Space Caper,* that tells of a rocket excursion into space. Each separate part of the story goes as follows:

Track 26: The rocket revs its engines and lifts off. The effect of the rocket's roaring engine is created with bunches of notes (CLUSTERS) played back and forth by the two hands. To add to the roaring sound, the notes are blurred together with the damper pedal. Only white keys are used for now, with the black keys being saved for a special effect, later.

Track 27: In a second stage, the rocket continues moving upward. The music from before is repeated in a higher register, moving farther up the keyboard.

Track 28 The rocket levels out, having arrived in space. The white key clusters hover around the same area, moving up a little, then back down a little, up a little, again, and then back down a little, once more.

Track 29: Strange and beautiful sights are seen. Now black keys are added to the white key clusters to give a new effect, and then a few chords and single notes are played in between, to tell this part of the story.

Track 30: The rocket returns peacefully home.
White-key clusters move back down the keyboard, until arriving back where they started from. Two soft notes played together at the very end, tell of the completion of the landing.

Track 31: contains the complete musical story.

Extra Fun: SOUND EFFECTS that you create can be added as you play your music. You might use common materials around you, effects from a midi keyboard, your own voice, or other such resources. The sounds can be created "live," as you play your musical story. Or, if you have a recording device, you can record your effects, then play your story along with them. Or, you can record your story, and then add the sound effects. There are a lot of fun ways to do this!

Track 32 adds midi sound effects to the musical story about the rocket.

Track 33 provides the sound effects alone, in case you wish to make up your own musical story along with these.

3-2-1 Lift-Off! Think of any subject you like, and begin playing some sounds to "tell your story."

Use any notes, pedals, and sound combinations you like, and "take off." Instead of notating all of your musical stories, you may wish to improvise many of them, and to memorize several, so that you can repeat them and perhaps add new material to them. With a friend, play stories for each other. Try to guess what each others' stories are about.

CD Track Index

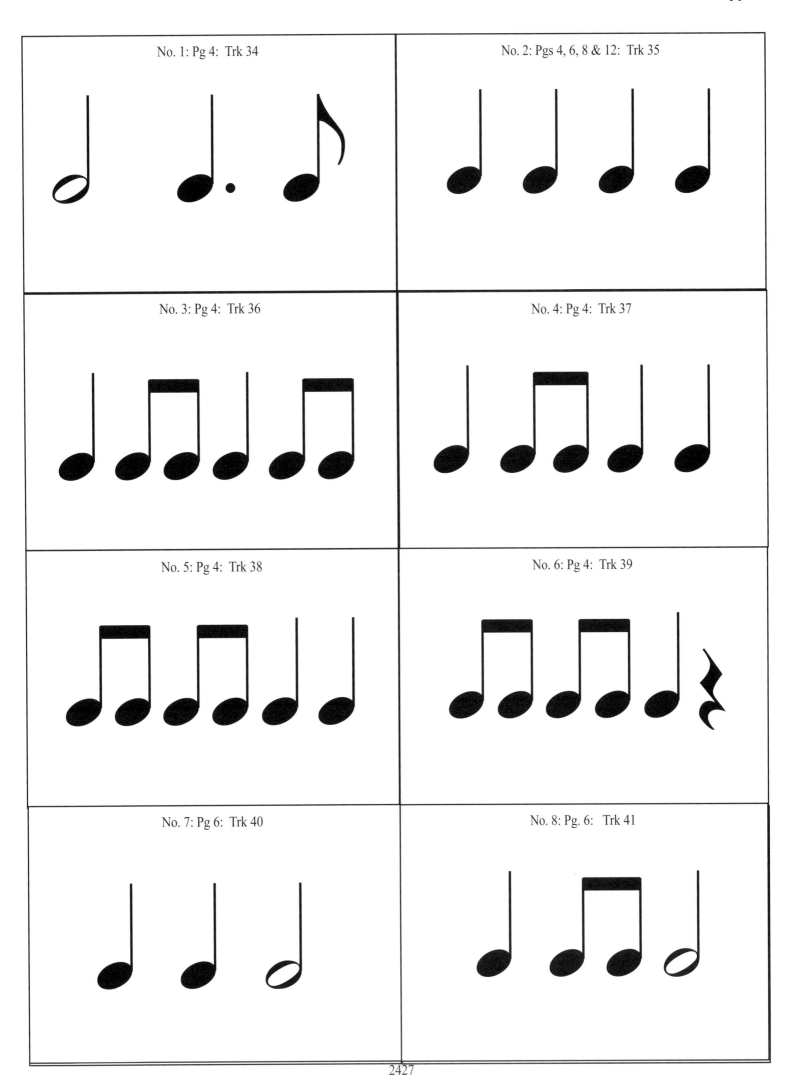

No. 2: Pgs 4, 6, 8 & 12: Trk 35	No. 1: Pg 4: Trk 34
♩ ♩ ♩ ♩	♩ ♩. ♪

No. 4: Pg 4: Trk 37	No. 3: Pg 4: Trk 36
♩ ♫♩ ♩	♩ ♩ ♫♩ ♫

No. 6: Pg 4: Trk 39	No. 5: Pg 4: Trk 38
♫ ♫♩ 𝄾	♫ ♫♩ ♩

No. 8: Pg. 6: Trk 41	No. 7: Pg 6: Trk 40
♩ ♫♩ ♩	♩ ♩ ♩

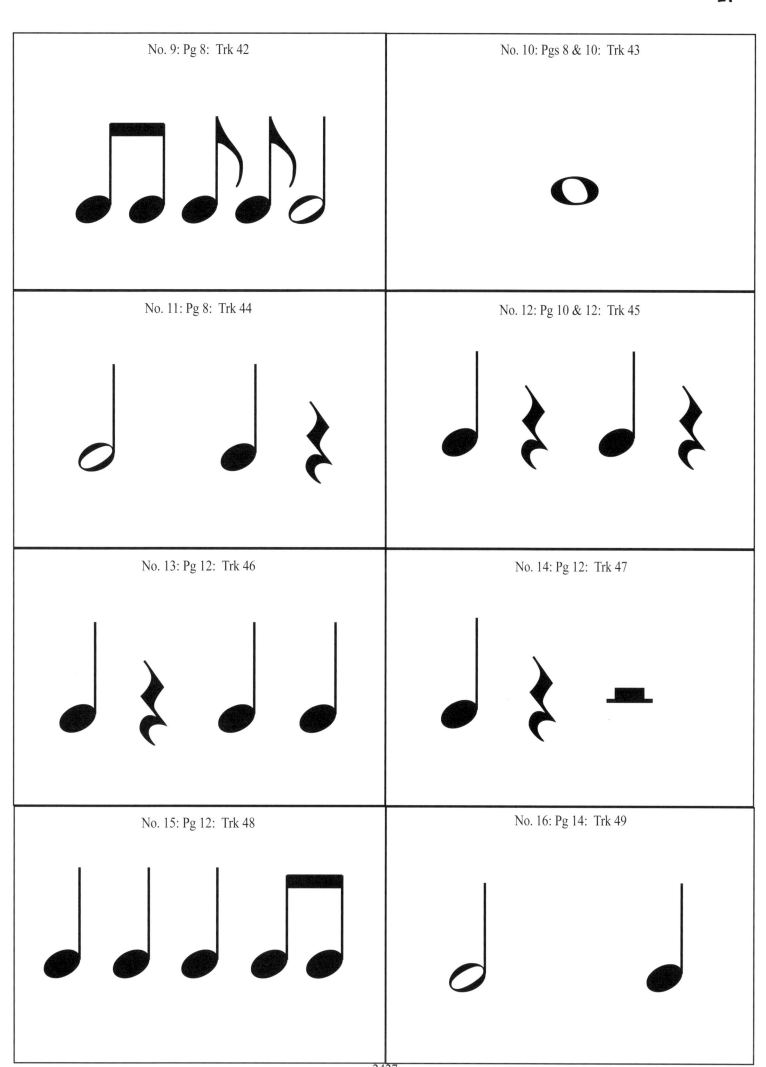

No. 9: Pg 8: Trk 42

No. 10: Pgs 8 & 10: Trk 43

No. 11: Pg 8: Trk 44

No. 12: Pg 10 & 12: Trk 45

No. 13: Pg 12: Trk 46

No. 14: Pg 12: Trk 47

No. 15: Pg 12: Trk 48

No. 16: Pg 14: Trk 49

No. 10: Pgs 8 & 10: Trk 43	No. 9: Pg 8: Trk 42
𝅝	♫♪♪♩
No. 12: Pg 10 & 12: Trk 45	**No. 11: Pg 8: Trk 44**
♩ 𝄾 ♩ 𝄾	♩ ♩ 𝄾
No. 14: Pg 12: Trk 47	**No. 13: Pg 12: Trk 46**
♩ 𝄾 —	♩ 𝄾 ♩ ♩
No. 16: Pg 14: Trk 49	**No. 15: Pg 12: Trk 48**
♩ ♩	♩ ♩ ♩ ♫

No. 17: Pg 17: Trk 50

No. 18: Pg 14: Trk 51

No. 19: Pgs 4-15

No. 18: Pg 14: Trk 51	No. 17: Pg 17: Trk 50
♩ ♩ ♩	♩.

No. 19: Pgs 4-15	
▬	